Té'Rana Aliyah

A BEAUTY WITH BRAINS

Shevonica M Howell

To order additional copies of this book, contact:
Xlibris
844-714-8691
www.Xlibris.com
Orders@Xlibris.com

ISBN: Softcover   978-1-6641-6725-4
        Hardcover   978-1-6641-6726-1
        EBook   978-1-6641-6724-7

Print information available on the last page

Rev. date: 04/06/2021

A BEAUTY WITH BRAINS

Te'Rana Aliyah

Te'Rana Aliyah is studying to be a Medical Assistant while working in the transportation field. She believes that she will be famous one day and she already possesses a love for shopping and fashion. Te'Rana has created a small business called Luxuriant Accessories. She sells unique purses, slippers and exotic lashes.

Unique Facts About Te'Rana:

Name:

Te'Rana Aliyah Austin

Birthdates:

September 18th (Jacksonville, Florida)

September 19th (Kaiserslautern, Germany)

Zodiac Sign:

VIRGO

Graduation Age & Date:

Graduated @16-years old … May 29th, 2019

Family Tree

Te'Rana Aliyah was born in Landstuhl, Germany, on September 19, 2002. She is the only daughter to her parents and she also has an older brother. Te'Rana also has an eight-year old niece and a three-year old nephew.

Fun Fact:

Te'Rana was born on Thursday, September 19, 2002, at approximately 1:03 a.m. Due to the time differences between Florida and Germany, if Te'Rana had been born in Jacksonville at that time ... her birthdate would have been Wednesday, September 18, 2002.

Gorgeous from Birth

Te'Rana was such a pretty baby and many would say that she should have auditioned to be in the Gerber baby commercials. Even as young as two-years old, she had a skin tone that looked as if she wore make-up on a daily basis. Her eyes and high cheek bones gave her the Naomi Campbell or Tyra Banks look on any occasion. Te'Rana always picked out her own clothes and she would get upset if she wanted ponytails instead of plats or braids with beads. Te'Rana was born to be a model and she enjoyed modeling for Sessions Modeling Agency in Jacksonville, Florida for a number of years.

Special Memory:

Te'Rana participated in an Annual Fashion Show presented by Sessions Modeling Agency at the Avenues Mall. She was the only 13-year old to participate.

Each of the other models were 18 years or older.

Making the Grades

When Te'Rana was 12-years old, she attended Academy of Scholars, Inc. during her middle school years. More importantly, she did extremely well on the school's standardized exams in both sixth and seventh grade and in turn, Te'Rana skipped the 8th grade and went on to 9th grade. Ironically, Te'Rana was also skipped to be a graduation ready senior after Winter Break in 2018. She became a high school graduate in 2019 after completing three online courses with Florida Virtual School (FLVS) and eight in-school courses that year at First Coast High School.

Interesting Fact:

Te'Rana became a Teacher's Assistant at 13-years old, a tutor to elementary students that same year, and she also had the pleasure of being an on-call tutor with a program funded by the Boys & Girls Club of Northwest Jacksonville.

Bitter Start ... Sweet Ending

Although Te'Rana skipped two years of school while attending private and public schools, she did not have the option of taking her senior yearbook pictures with the Class of 2019 or participate in senior "week" activities. But, Te'Rana did enjoy participating in the Senior Prom of 2019 as well as Grad Nite in Orlando. She indeed missed her friends that she grew up with from elementary to middle school, but the excitement of graduating just a month after Grad Nite ... made her happy!

Happy Memory:

Te'Rana & her prom date

ended the night sailing on

a Yacht from Ortega River Marina...

Dress & Suit Designed by:

Michelle @ IG: WhyBoutique
(904)894-4094

Male Shoes:

Neiman Marcus
Ms. Esmeralda Castaneda
(Peachtree Mall Atlanta)

Photos by:

Bracy Photos
bracyphotos.as.me
Edward Denson Studios
(904)601-9221

Yacht Services by:

Captain Kevin
FirstCoastCharters.com
(904)270-9463

Fun Facts:

Te'Rana received her learner's permit at 15-years old by passing her very first online driver's exam. She managed to purchase two cars by 16 and at 18, Te'Rana took over insurance payments to drive her Mother's 2015 Kia.

The Good Outweighs the Bad

As a teenager, Te'Rana struggled with finding her own identity and many times it was at the expense of making her parents feel that she was less appreciative than grateful for her many blessings. Being that Te'Rana's parents divorced during her elementary years in school, it is safe to say that the stress of the divorce alone affected her in more ways than one. And like many kids and young adults, acting out was the norm when trying to cope. There were times when Te'Rana showed signs of depression, anger, disrespect and even a dislike for both parents, but with counseling and love from those that loved her ... the positive outweighed the negative.

Factual Synopsis:

Te'Rana loves being around family and friends, but when she needs time alone...GIVE IT TO HER! Ironically, Te'Rana completed a personality test in 9th grade and her results indicated that she has introverted, observant, thinking and prospecting personality traits.

She agreed with the results 100%.

Her Ultimate Goals

Te'Rana graduated high school at 16-years old on Wednesday, May 29, 2019. She was anxious to start college immediately and applied at Florida State College at Jacksonville. After not doing as well as she had wished in the three courses she signed up for, Te'Rana took a sabbatical from college. At this time, Te'Rana is enrolled in a Medical Assistant program at a local college and she is working a 9 to 5 position doing something she love ... DRIVING!

Te'Rana plans to revamp her business, Luxuriant Accessories, continue working her 9 to 5, complete the Medical Assistant program within the year and become a Merchant Seaman in the future.

Her Favoites

HER MOTTO

One Step at a Time

HER FAVORITE SONG

He Saw the Best in Me

HER FAVORITE FOOD

Shrimp Alfredo

HER FAVORITE RESTAURANT

Juicy Crab

HER FAVORITE COLOR:

Pink

Introducing Te'Rana Aliyah Austin

Written Especially for Te'Rana

She's All Mine & the love I have for her is a love that I never knew existed.

She looks like me, is the exact same size as me (back in my day), but she is nothing like me.

Her get up and go demeanor! Her zeal for life! And her no holds bar attitude is refreshing to say the least.

If only I had the discernment that she has when I was her age ... Shoot! No one would be able to stop me!

Her drive for greatness is the mere reason that I know she will remain unstoppable.

She's advanced amongst her peers, her sibling and her foes. She's that pretty girlie-girl today, the tomboy that you love to hate tomorrow and the forever party-girl that you will continue to love if she allowed it.

To think about it, it is extremely exhausting to wonder about the deep dark thoughts that she has inside. And if I didn't know her ... know her, I'm sure that being afraid of her would be my only option.

She takes chances! She seems to never be afraid of adversity! She is a true go-getter, she's not shy and will tell you quick ... when she has changed her mind!

If she didn't like something ... you would know it.

And if she wanted things to change, you would know that as well. Her confidence

and the pride that she displays on a daily basis, continue to give me life!

She's my girl and for that I am loved. She's my girl and for that I am never alone.

She's my girl and forever I will cherish her.

She's Mine & to know her is love!

Dear God, thanks for my "one and only"
beautiful & intelligent daughter... ☺

Glossary

beauty – a combination of qualities, such as shape, color or form, that pleases the aesthetic senses, especially the sight.

confidence – the feeling or belief that one can rely on someone or something; firm trust.

depression – a mental health disorder that causes feelings of sadness and/or a loss of interest in activities.

discernment – the ability to judge well.

divorce – the legal dissolution of a marriage by a court or other competent body.

fashion show – an event at which collections of newly designed clothing are modeled for an audience.

goals – the object of a person's ambition or effort; an aim or desired result.

Medical Assistant – a person trained to assist medical professionals.

model – a person who poses to display clothing, either on stage or in photographs.

motto – a slogan or favorite saying.

personality test – a method of assessing human personality constructs.

prom – a formal dance held by a high school at the end of the academic year, typical for students in their junior or senior year.

standardized test – a test (as of intelligence, achievement, or personality) whose reliability has been established by obtaining an average score of a significantly large number of individuals for use as a standard of comparison.

Teacher's Assistant – a student tasked with the responsible of assisting an instructor with grading papers, assisting students with tutoring, etc.

tutor – a person charged with the instruction and guidance of another.

Virgo – the sixth sign of the zodiac in astrology. Virgos are logical, practical, and systematic in their approach in life.

Spelling Assignment

Directions: Use the Glossary to unscramble the following words.

1. r o v g i _____

2. t o m o t _____

3. o u t r t _____

4. s e d p s e o n r i _____

5. r p m o _____

6. e t y u b a _____

7. e m d l o _____

8. g l s o a _____

9. s a f o n i h w s o h _____

10. c r e s d n t m n i e _____

11. v o e d r i c _____

12. f e o c n i e d n c _____

Reading Assignment

1. Who is the Author of this book? _____

2. What publishing company published this book? _____

3. Define confidence _____

_____

4. What year did Te'Rana graduate from high school? _____

5. _____ is the ability to judge well.

6. What is Te'Rana's favorite color? _____

7. Does Te'Rana have any siblings? _____

8. Is it true that Te'Rana has two nieces and two nephews? Yes or No _____

9. Where was Te'Rana born? _____

10. List two interesting facts about Te'Rana _____

_____

11. What Modeling Agency was Te'Rana affiliated with and at what age? _____

12. List something about this book that you really enjoyed and explain why you enjoyed it. _____ _____

_____

_____

13. Is there anything that you did not like about this book? Explain _____

_____

14. List two goals that you would like to accomplish before the end of this year.

_____

_____

_____

_____

15. What is your favorite color? _____

Word Search

divorce   tutor   Virgo   beauty   motto   model

prom   depression   discernment   confidence   personality test   goals

fashion show   Teacher Assistant   Medical Assistant   standardized exam

m	e	d	i	c	a	l	a	s	s	i	s	t	a	n	t
a	j	w	q	k	q	u	b	v	e	k	d	e	o	x	m
h	t	s	e	t	y	t	i	l	a	n	o	s	r	e	p
b	x	n	g	a	j	o	n	p	q	w	i	c	f	j	z
y	d	e	p	r	e	s	s	i	o	n	v	e	s	l	g
t	e	a	c	h	e	r	a	s	s	i	s	t	a	n	t
u	c	r	w	y	c	t	d	w	r	e	p	c	q	v	u
a	g	m	o	d	e	l	h	g	f	g	r	t	j	m	t
e	s	f	a	s	h	i	o	n	s	h	o	w	y	g	o
b	q	c	z	m	t	n	j	b	q	z	m	l	f	p	r
d	i	v	o	r	c	e	g	x	e	s	k	a	g	c	e
z	h	t	e	n	l	o	a	s	r	c	b	n	s	i	d
s	t	a	n	d	a	r	d	i	z	e	d	e	x	a	m
o	f	d	p	l	c	o	n	f	i	d	e	n	c	e	h
n	g	j	s	d	i	s	c	e	r	n	m	e	n	t	p

Books From This Author

Girl, they Ain't ready! (2011)

I CAN DIG IT SIS … THEY AIN'T READY! (2017)

What's in a Name? (2018)

A Play with Words Word Search Book (2020)

The "YOU TEACH IT" Math Study Guide (2020)

We Love You, Dre! (2021)

A is for Audre' (2021)

FINDING MYSELF … AM I ENOUGH? (2021)

Printed in the United States
by Baker & Taylor Publisher Services